LONDON LIVING

LONDON LIVING

TOWN AND COUNTRY

SIMON UPTON

VENDOME

NEW YORK · LONDON

CONTENTS

FOREWORD Nicky Haslam 12
INTRODUCTION Simon Upton 15

LONDON 23

HUNTER GATHERER 24
Hubert Zandberg, Spitalfields

INFLUENTIAL GLAMOUR 32
Poppy Delevingne, Shepherd's Bush

RACONTEUR 38
Adam Bray, St John's Wood

ENIGMA 44
Bella Freud, North Kensington

ART & DESIGN 52
Francis Upritchard and Martino Gamper, Hackney

DESIGN DUO 58
Joanna and Nick Plant, Acton

GRANDEE 68
John Stefanidis, Belgravia

ARTIST IN RESIDENCE 80
Kate Braine, Chelsea

INTERIOR DRESSERS 94
Christopher De Vos and Peter Pilotto, De Beauvoir Town

RETHINKERS 100
Maria Speake and Adam Hills, Marylebone

MAN ABOUT TOWN 112
Tomasz Starzewski, South Kensington

CREATIVE WORKS 122
Tom Bartlett, North Kensington

RESTRAINED 128
William Smalley, Bloomsbury

RAREFIED CURIOSITIES 138
Emma Hawkins, Notting Hill

LONDON + COUNTRY 147

ACQUIRING MINDS 148
Alastair and Megan Holberton, Kensington And Oxfordshire

ADVENTURERS 166
Blake and Chad Pike, Chelsea And Wiltshire

CURATORS 190
David Gibson and Jorge Perez-Martin, Chelsea and Gloucestershire

STORYTELLERS 204
Gaby Dellal and David Johnson, Notting Hill and Cornwall

FREE SPIRIT 220
Jane Ormsby Gore, Kilburn and Wales

AESTHETE 234
Jasper Conran, Bayswater and Dorset

THE COLLECTORS' COLLECTOR 260
Belgravia and Norfolk

INFORMED 280
Roger Jones and Gregory Chambers, Chelsea and Wales

CLASS ACT 294
Tish Weinstock and Tom Guinness, Holland Park and Wiltshire

ACKNOWLEDGEMENTS 318
PICTURE CREDITS 319

FOREWORD

One would be perfectly justified in believing that Simon has never heard of
electric light. He certainly has little need of it: no reflective boards, no silver-
lined umbrellas, no cunning spots, placed just so, encumber his equipage.
He simply enters a room, sees a chink of natural light, and by some sleight
of eye, explodes that gleam into a galaxy, illuminating the space with pin-
point accuracy of hue, nuance and unforced romance.

Originally studying to be a painter – Simon comes from a family of artists
– he soon became enthralled with photography, initially portraiture, while
absorbing what he calls 'the otherliness' of colour and curve, shape and
surfaces, in artefacts and architecture. The combination evolved into his
distinct gift as a portrayer of our inhabited spaces, from the simplest to the
grandest: the photographs herein are his bestilled yet vibrant interpretation
of that lovely 'otherliness'.

Simon studied at Farnham College of Art & Design, a cultural haven amid
Surrey's many military establishments; but Simon – long-legged with a neat
head – does have the bearing and ordered mentality of an army officer. One
can picture him on the Khyber Pass in pale khaki, riding into darkened chasms
with, of course, only the stars as his guide.

So, when he turns up for a shoot, barehanded but for a camera and a laptop
– no calls for coffee, no stops for sandwiches – one senses immediately that
the day is won. And that's before he's found the sliver of light with which to
illuminate the images in *London Living*: proof positive that, with his eclectic
vision, rooms do most surely furnish a book.

INTRODUCTION

SIMON UPTON

If I were to be asked whether I consider myself a town or a country person, I would have to say 'country', having moved to Devon from London a decade ago. Prior to that, I lived and worked in London for more than thirty years and will always consider it as my base, if not necessarily my home.

The joy of my profession as an interiors and lifestyle photographer is the daily discovery of the unexpected and wonderful places that people call 'home'; the variety, richness and creativity that exists in London takes my breath away, and I never lose my sense of excitement as I head off to a new location each morning.

Perhaps deliberately, this book, which follows the success of *New York Interiors*, does not reflect the many beautiful homes in London that have been created for other people by some of the world's most talented interior designers. These properties have been well documented already, and I have been privileged to photograph many of them over the years. The designers, antiques dealers and artists listed below have helped to shape me as a photographer and, more importantly, have become my friends. In acknowledgement and gratitude, this introduction is therefore dedicated to all of you, both past and present: Roger Banks-Pye, Christopher Gibbs, Robert Kime, Rose Uniacke, Will and Charlotte Fisher, Peter Hone, Veere Grenney, Wendy Nicholls, Nicky Haslam, Chester Jones, Tricia Guild, Nina Campbell, David Mlinaric, Hugh Henry, Tino Zervudachi and Flora Soames.

Your inspirational interiors have regularly graced the pages of *The World of Interiors* and *House & Garden*, magazines to which I owe my career as a photographer. A huge debt of gratitude to Min Hogg and Rupert Thomas, past and present editors at *The World of Interiors*, and Sue Crewe and Hatta Byng, past and present editors at *House & Garden*. Without regular exposure in their magazines, I would never have got to know any of you – the people who influence the trends in interior design today. My final thanks go to my great and lasting friends, Liza Bruce and Nicholas Alvis Vega.

Continued page 21 >

RIGHT
The iconic blue and white bedroom
of the late Roger Banks-Pye of
Colefax & Fowler.

BELOW
Rose Uniacke's London kitchen.

ABOVE
The late Robert Kime's London
sitting room.

OPPOSITE
Liza Bruce's and Nicholas Alvis Vega's
country bedroom.

The double living room in Will and
Charlotte Fisher's London home.

RIGHT
A glimpse of Peter Hone's extraordinary
collection in his London apartment.

RIGHT
A bathroom in Will and Charlotte
Fisher's London home.

In order to explore the meaning of 'home', the importance of which has been evident since Covid forced the world into lockdown, I decided to focus on interiors with a deeply personal feel. They range from Hackney and Spitalfields in the east, to Marylebone and Bloomsbury, Belgravia, Chelsea, Kensington, Notting Hill and Acton further west. Few have appeared in print before, and all have been created with love, reverence and a gloriously individual aesthetic. As Nicky Haslam cleverly puts it: 'Style is the bit that doesn't come out of a tin. You can acquire taste and discover what is tasteful, but style is a personal statement that only works for the individual.'

I see homes as portraits of the people who live in them, whether they are owned or rented. As such, I have tried to illustrate the importance of place as well as the quintessential Englishness that is often so evident. Yet, in juxtaposition to this, London is also a fantastic melting pot of nationalities and cultures, which has a major influence on the way people live. In order to reflect this – and maintain the dynamic of each private space as it appeared when I first walked through the door – nothing has been altered in the interiors I have photographed.

The second part of this book features the homes of those people who also have houses in the country. My aim in this section was to show the similarities – themes, colours, furnishings – that tie the places together. As was the case with the London interiors, the country homes were dotted about; I went to Wales, Norfolk, Wiltshire, Cornwall and several counties in between. All were fabulous and served to compound my appreciation of the diversity of the British landscape. How lucky we are to live in a country where there are so many different places we can call 'home'.

LONDON

As an Englishman I have an abiding appreciation of the country I grew up in; as an interiors photographer I have spent the past thirty years attempting to capture the idiosyncrasies of style and design that, for me, are the essence of Englishness.

London Living reveals the diversity, eccentricity, humour and individuality I have discovered in so many English homes. Inspired by the variety of architecture in London, each of the interiors I have photographed, be they grand or modest, reveals a passion for design and an understanding of colour, composition and comfort.

I have always had a base in London and, like many city dwellers, have upgraded when circumstances allowed. My greatest find came in the early 1990s when I was looking for a New York-style loft space as a live-work environment. They were as rare as hen's teeth in those days, with developers buying up empty buildings to gut and turn into small flats to satisfy the ever-increasing demand for new housing.

As luck would have it, I discovered a brick warehouse with a small number of studio spaces for sale in an unfashionable area between Notting Hill and Maida Vale, known as Maida Hill. The warehouse was nothing more than a double-height empty shell with a pitched roof and its own front door. The moment I walked in I could see how to make the most of the volume and light – and I bought it on the spot!

When I got married and had my daughter, the idea of living in the country became increasingly appealing. Eventually, I exchanged my loft for a restoration project in Devon that has kept us occupied for the past ten years. I felt the loss of a London base keenly, however, so my wife and I started looking for a little 'lock-up-and-leave' flat.

My happy memories of living in Notting Hill, in addition to its proximity to Heathrow airport (I travel a lot for work), meant that we focused our search on my old neighbourhood. The flat we found was on the first floor of a Victorian stucco terrace house and had high ceilings and original plasterwork. It needed refurbishing, so we gutted it in order to transform it into a beautifully simple living space with wooden floors and a marble fireplace.

Because I am so often away, the feeling of coming home – be it opening the door to our London flat or hearing the crunch of gravel under my car tyres as I arrive at our country house – is particularly poignant. It is always a relief to return to my refuge.

HUNTER GATHERER

HUBERT ZANDBERG, SPITALFIELDS

London is the centre of the world – things happen here! I arrived from South Africa in 1997 when the energy of the art scene had been transformed by the YBAs (Young British Artists), whose work appeared in *Sensation*, an exhibition at the Royal Academy.

Travel is in my DNA. Over the years I have acquired homes in London, Berlin, Paris and Cape Town, cities with which I feel a strong affinity. One of the reasons I invest in property is because it gives me a new playground in which to indulge my passion for creating dialogues between objects and art. I have been buying art all my life which means that much of my collection has had to go into storage.

I have lived in London for twenty-seven years and have come to love it. I remember the precise day I felt like a Londoner and the city became home. It was like a religious experience. I have always bought or rented in West London yet was intrigued by Spitalfields because of its heavy dose of history – it is so redolent of old London. Ironically, the flat I bought is a wolf in sheep's clothing: a mock Georgian new build from the 1990s in a street of period houses.

The design of the flat, which is tiny, was driven by the art I had decided to hang. It is the ultimate jewellery box; I wanted it to be a representation of my old home on Ladbroke Grove, my first true cabinet of curiosities. I made the space look bigger by adding more and more stuff, which emphasises the fact that it is just a box, a little 'Wunderkammer'. The scale makes sense, yet it is also a comfortable place to stay with a big bed, a huge shower and an oversized sofa.

During the three years it took to renovate, the flat became a laboratory for some of the design schemes my team and I were working on: the terrazzo floor and paint techniques in the kitchen and lobby were all experiments, as was the plaster mould on the living room ceiling, which we were trying out for the bathrooms of a beach project.

I wanted the space to take on the character of a painting. It was a very considered design; every surface is covered – nothing is left as plaster or brick. The walls are either lined with fabric, or panelled, in a nod to traditional jewellery boxes which are upholstered in velvet, satin, leather or veneer, all with beautiful detailing.

My favourite part of any design is hanging the art at the end. Although each of the rooms in this flat were contrived around paintings I had already chosen for them, the luxurious burnt-orange velvet on the walls of the living room – so beautiful and simple – made me unusually hesitant.

For now, London is where I spend most of my time, but nothing is permanent.

INFLUENTIAL GLAMOUR

POPPY DELEVINGNE, SHEPHERD'S BUSH

I am a Londoner, born and bred. I grew up in Wandsworth, south-west of the Thames. As a child I was convinced that the Queen lived in one of the little huts at either end of Albert Bridge, the prettiest bridge in London, especially at night when it's illuminated by strings of single light bulbs that look like a pearl necklace.

My childhood home was located right on Wandsworth Common in an area known locally as the 'Toast Rack'. We lived in a street full of large Victorian houses, some of which had blue plaques on them to commemorate famous residents. The blue plaques scheme was started in 1866 by English Heritage. In our neck of the woods, one of the plaques is dedicated to David Lloyd George, who was Prime Minister during the First World War.

London has more parks, gardens, common land and green spaces than any other city I have visited and Wandsworth Common, with its tall trees, secret hiding places, ponds and lake full of wildlife, is no exception. My childhood memories, which I share with my sisters Chloe and Cara, are of wild, carefree days climbing trees and getting our knees grubby! Wandsworth was such a great place to live that I didn't move out of my parents' house until I was well into my twenties. When I got married in 2014, I was determined to find something similar.

I ended up moving north of the river, to a tree-lined street in Shepherd's Bush, a residential neighbourhood in West London. We discovered the house through word of mouth. Although it was only the second place we looked at, we knew immediately that it would be perfect. Achieving the perfection we were after called for major refurbishment, however. The building works took more than a year during which time, with the help of an architect, we relocated the central staircase, raised and lowered ceilings and excavated the garden. At one point I remember standing in what had become a shell of the house we had bought and being able to see all the way from the basement to the roof!

The interiors of our favourite rooms are inspired by our travels. For example, the sitting room with its glossy walls and velvet curtains was influenced by Hotel Costes in Paris. The one room that was non-negotiable for me in terms of decoration was the bedroom. All I ever wanted was a pink bedroom – calming in summer and cocoon-like in winter.

Home is everything to me. It is where my heart is, the place where I feel fully myself. Over the years I have been lucky enough to experience, and live in, many cities around the world, but London is where I belong. When I am away, I miss the vibrancy, the culture, the energy and the familiarity. I can't imagine not chatting to taxi drivers about the weather, or going to my local pub, or breathing in the smell of wet pavements which, for me, is the thing I love most about London.

RACONTEUR

ADAM BRAY, ST JOHN'S WOOD

I was born in London and grew up on Marylebone Road in a big Victorian mansion block near the Tube station. Most of the residents were old ladies, now long since gone. I lived with my grandmother, who had a hairdressing salon nearby where I would wait to be collected after school. I used to while away the time by looking at copies of *Country Life*, *Vogue* and *Cosmopolitan* which gave me a slightly unusual perception of what adult life might promise.

As a child I wanted to be a photographer, but I was so technically inept I couldn't hold down a job. Instead, when I was seventeen, I started working at Denton Antiques on Marylebone High Street, where I stayed for a year before moving to Delomosne, an antiques dealer on Campden Hill Road. Delomosne specialises in glass and porcelain and my first job was to unpack and wash the pieces. It was an amazingly hands-on way of learning how to look at objects – checking things over, looking for repairs – and an invaluable start.

My transition from antiques dealer to interior decorator was entirely due to a small shop on Ledbury Road in Notting Hill. I was twenty-four and precocious. Danny Katz, an art dealer, helped me to secure the lease and several antiques dealers, including Edric van Vredenburgh and Piers von Westenholz, were very supportive.

My childhood home was immaculate and considered, but we rarely had parties and there were few visitors. I've tried to make up for it in my own home. I love preparing the flat for a party and to have people sitting around swapping dealers' stories and staying up late!

I have been in this flat for many years. It's rented from a friend with whom I have worked for the past twenty years. I have two sons who hang out here a lot, so it's as much a place for family as a quiet space for me to work, which probably adds to the feeling of 'organised chaos'.

The building comprises three flats, with a studio at the back, which was once owned by the artist and sculptor Sir Frank Dicksee. In the 1890s it would have been an entire house and the area where it sits, like Chelsea, considered a haven for artists.

Originally, this flat was divided into bedsits, but my landlady knocked the two together, which is great as it means I have large spaces to live and work in and the luxury of two open fireplaces, a rarity in central London.

My home is my refuge. The furniture is comfortable; the lighting is low and shadowy; and there is always music playing from my cobbled-together music system.

I love living in London: the hustle, the diversity, the privacy and the strange relationships that develop over the years with people at the local shops, from the dry cleaner to the greengrocer. Then there is the Parcel Force delivery guy, who leaves detailed notes about the latest football results on the 'Sorry I missed you' card he puts through my letter box!

ENIGMA

BELLA FREUD, NORTH KENSINGTON

I was born on Ladbroke Grove in North Kensington. My mother lived in a block of flats set back from the road, and I have been in this part of London for most of my life, not counting a blip in the 1980s when I moved east. When I was growing up, I never felt that we had a place of our own. My mother and I did not live with my father, and I always seemed to be in other people's houses.

During my teenage years, I went to fashion school and worked for Vivienne Westwood in her shop, before creating my own label. I started with knitwear and accessories and have never stopped.

I have always shopped around Portobello Road where there is a good clothes and antiques market on Fridays. I would often go down there 'just looking'. Sadly, most of the vintage shops along the Golborne Road have long since gone, but what is lovely is that the stall holders all recognise me, not in an intrusive way, but because I am a regular. There is such a great sense of community in London.

My now ex-husband, James, and I discovered this building through a connection with the original owners, casting director Camilla Arthur and Mark Lebon, and we bought the flat above this one some years ago. It was quiet, tumbling down and needed a lot of work; James still lives upstairs. I eventually bought this site out the back, which is where the interior designer Willie Nickerson used to live. It was literally all asbestos! We had to demolish everything and then design what is fundamentally a landlocked site from a series of makeshift studios.

I turned to Maria Speake of Retrouvius for help. Maria and I work really well together – she always has great ideas and is the only interior architect I have ever collaborated with. The main problem was the total lack of windows, as it meant we had to put in skylights, which determined how the design came together. Since the only way to get light in was from above, we put in lots of internal 'windows' in order to create a visual connection through the building.

Maria is incredibly good with proportion and flow and suggested a kind of interior courtyard using layers of different greens to create a garden-like living area, something I would never have thought of. I knew the design was fancier than I had first imagined but I didn't have any other ideas at the time and the result is fantastic. What is also great is that although I am living in the centre of West London, I cannot see my neighbours and the only view I have is of the sky.

As a fashion designer, I like to think that I am good with colour. This flat slightly reminds me of a New York loft and I wanted to paint it in a kind of 1970s white instead of the Empire Grey I have been eternally obsessed with. From the many shades of white we tried, the one that actually looked grey was the one that worked with the London light filtering in from above!

The idea of home has always been a really big deal for me. This is the nicest place I have ever lived in – I am surrounded by walls, which is comforting and safe, and I have made it just how I want it. Good design can change your life!

ART & DESIGN

FRANCIS UPRITCHARD AND MARTINO GAMPER, HACKNEY

In the 1990s London was exciting. Everything was happening here – music, fashion, design, multi-culturalism … London was a melting pot of great talent.

I finished art school in New Zealand in 1998 and couldn't wait to leave. My sculpting was going well but I knew I needed to struggle more, so I headed to London. I couldn't afford college, so I spent my time going to shows and exhibitions and ran the Bart Wells Institute with Luke Gottelier – a space for artists – as a way of educating myself. Being cashless in a city like London could have been much more difficult than it was, but I could sense that life in London was going to be good.

I had seen a poster for a preliminary show of Martino's work – his 100 Chairs in 100 Days project – at The Design Museum. I missed the show but was keen to meet him, so I tracked him down to this building; we got on immediately.

Martino came to London from Milan at around the same time as I had arrived from New Zealand. He did an exchange at the Royal College of Art (RCA), after which he applied to stay on. He was living in the Clapton Depot – a warehouse space up the road from here – when he heard from some fellow RCA students that there was a vacancy in this building. In 2005 he moved into a derelict flat on the first floor and within three months had transformed it into a studio/workshop.

One day, the tenant renting the ground floor did a runner. The strange noises heard at night turned out to have been him printing fake money. Suddenly, the floor below us was a big empty space with a few bits of abandoned machinery lying around. It clearly had huge potential and the rent was very cheap, so Martino took it on even though it was freezing and there was

no natural light. Gradually, he improved it and built a self-contained workshop.

As a tenant, there is always the threat of eviction, so when the chance to buy this building came up, we went for it, helped by an unexpected interest from a sculptor and his wife who were old friends. Between us, we managed to scrape together the money before the building was sacrificed to a far less appropriate redevelopment.

Ownership of a semi-derelict property created new problems, and early on in its renovation we decided to add two floors and create three equal-sized flats, one of which is our home. Everything here is built of pre-cut, solid wood panels and was assembled on the spot – a prefab house. It's a really ecological way of building – and within ten days the structure of the house was complete.

While our spiritual homes are in Italy and New Zealand with our respective families, our physical home and creative hub is in London. Art is hugely important to us, and we continue to collaborate with other artists, jewellers, potters, weavers and glassblowers.

DESIGN DUO

JOANNA AND NICK PLANT, ACTON

When we first saw this house a little more than twenty years ago, it wasn't an obvious choice. Built in the late 1920s, it had no redeeming features except for the enormous garden, which is what sealed the deal for us. With two young sons, space for them to scratch about with sticks was what we needed most, and over the years we have grown vegetables, kept bantams and now, in its most grown-up iteration, we have a parterre rose garden, where I often spend the very early morning, wandering around with a cup of tea.

Acton is only a few miles west of Notting Hill, which was experiencing a special time in the 1990s. Nick, who learned everything from his mentor Goerge Sherlock, had a shop, Succession, on Westbourne Grove, close to other furniture shops like Themes & Variations, B&T Antiques and David Champion. I was making the first inroads into interior design at that time – my background is not an obvious one – and being part of Nick's world was the best immersion I could have wished for.

Over the years, our house has evolved to reflect our requirements as a family. There was never a conscious plan in its redesign, but there was a sense of where we wanted to end up. In the early years, we focused on opening up the house to include spaces for entertaining. The original building stopped at the back of the kitchen where the back door opened onto the garden. The dining room replaced a car port with a corrugated plastic roof, and we rearranged the orientation of some of the doors to change the flow of the rooms. Nick has always been a furniture-maker and antiques dealer, which means that the pieces at home ebb and flow according to both a desire for change as well as to keep things interesting.

I am not a huge fan of open plan spaces; I like rooms that are defined by their function. That function has evolved, just as we have as a family, and whether the boys are living with us or not: bedrooms become dressing rooms; studies become libraries; and storage rooms become larders. The downstairs loo has been opened up and turned into a rather grand laundry room, with ticking curtains and tongue-and-groove panelling – probably my favourite room at the moment.

This house was rather unimpressive back then, but it has been generous to us over the years, allowing us to make it into something more interesting and, ultimately, a real family home.

GRANDEE

JOHN STEFANIDIS, BELGRAVIA

Apart from Ebury Street, I have had two other houses in London: in Chester Square, the top two floors were gutted to make a double-height studio with a gallery, and Cheyne Walk, a more intellectually satisfying house with its eighteenth-century architecture and its history as the headquarters of the Moravians in London. To begin with I only had one floor – the *piano nobile*, made famous by the movie *Blow Out*. I bought the rest by degrees and improved the Lutyens garden hugely, made bathrooms and comfortable spaces.

Cheyne Walk was at its best when there was a party, the rooms being used to their full potential with guests spilling out into the garden. I had Cock Crow, my house in Dorset, at the same time but, after twenty years, both houses having given me much pleasure, the time had come to sell them, which I did in the same year.

I spent more time at my house in Greece and bought the one shown here. Originally, the one on Ebury Street belonged to a watchmaker, who would sit on a bench by the window in the front room to make the most of the available daylight.

Before moving into a smaller property, a friend asked, 'Are you going to be one of those old men with a house full of clutter?' Well, it is full of clutter, but of a special kind, and is the antithesis to my house on Patmos, which I have had for more than fifty years, and which has remained empty but beautiful.

I enjoyed Cock Crow and the country very much: it was simple. When I look at photographs of barns and conversions, I always think too much has been done to them. I did the minimum at Cock Crow so that it would not lose its integrity as cow sheds – only cows had lived there – no vicars, no ghosts, no scandals, no unhappy spinsters who haunt so many old houses.

Ebury Street is my pied-à-terre in life. Perhaps I feel this way because I am not English but Alexandrian Greek and essentially an exile from a world that no longer exists.

When I moved from the country, I sold much of my furniture I felt was not right or too big for Ebury Street – interestingly there was little I wished to keep. The house is convenient in every way, and the garden a breath of fresh air which has parakeets and over thirty other species of birds as daily visitors.

ARTIST IN RESIDENCE

KATE BRAINE, CHELSEA

I was brought up in Chelsea, so I really am a local. My parents lived in Cheyne Walk, a few streets from here. I love the proximity to the Thames. Despite its popularity with foreign buyers, Chelsea has never lost its association with the artists who once lived here. It was once a great potting area: Chelsea China, a soft-paste porcelain manufacturer was established around the corner in Lawrence Street in 1743, and the William De Morgan tile factory, which was set up in 1872, was also nearby.

We bought this Queen Anne house twenty-six years ago. It was our physical home until seven years ago when we acquired one of those magnificent studios in Glebe Place, three minutes' walk away. This place will always be my spiritual home, though, because it's where the children grew up. I still spend the night here sometimes, reliving some of the family's most special moments and creating new ones in my studio at the bottom of the garden.

In addition to my memories, home, for me, is about the things I have collected on my travels, the furniture that has been handed down to me by my grandparents and parents and, increasingly, my 'pots'.

I went to art school and studied sculpture. I am classically trained, so I did life and body casting and was taught to do portraits of heads, all with a plumb line and callipers.

I was commissioned by all sorts of people, many of whom were well known at the time and many who went on to become even more famous. When I was nineteen, I did a body cast of David Bowie. He had to wear a black dustbin liner as a skirt ... plaster dropping everywhere. It was hilarious, and he was charming! After that, we did a sculpture together – I cast it in bronze, David added a mask and then had a solo show in Cork Street.

I find that splitting my time between both properties is very good for my brain. It's lovely to leave home and come here to work. I don't run this place as a full-time house, but I do try and use it for the good of other artists by opening it for exhibitions of pottery and ceramics. The shows do really well because, I think, there is a magical feel here which you don't find in a gallery.

I am so pleased I didn't sell this place. You don't know what you have got until you consider letting it go. The memories, the family, the resonance ... they simply could not be recreated in another house.

INTERIOR DRESSERS

CHRISTOPHER DE VOS AND PETER PILOTTO, DE BEAUVOIR TOWN

Overlooking Regent's Canal in East London with an amazing view of the city beyond, this Art Deco building was extended in 2008 to create eight flats on the top. As locals, we already knew – and loved – the exterior, so it was extremely lucky that this apartment became available in 2011 at the time we were looking to move. The few photographs we saw showed it to be really unusual. The architect turned out to be Claudio Silvestrin – it was his show flat – whose aesthetic is the polar opposite to ours.

Although we were never going to adopt Claudio's way of living, there are aspects of his signature style we love, including the void which creates a double-height ceiling and the beautiful washbasin and shower upstairs which is made of a rough porphyry that he always uses. We also like the hidden storage, sliding doors and the use of beautiful wood.

In early 2020, after we decided to take a break from designing for our fashion label, Peter Pilotto, and travel through South America, Covid happened and we got stuck in the countryside in Ecuador for months, which gave us time to think about the future.

We missed our home in London and being surrounded by all the things we have collected over the years. On our return, we repainted the entire flat and reupholstered the sofa, which is when the idea of creating textiles for the home really started. Peter Pilotto is known for its prints, jacquards and embroideries, and the transition from fashion to interiors has felt like a natural progression for us. Our flat has become a place in which to experiment with the durability and sustainability of fabrics as well as the mix of patterns and colours.

I think our love of colour and graphics has a lot to do with our mixed heritage. Peter is Austro-Italian, and I am half Peruvian and half Belgian. A reference to nature is also an important part of our design process – the malachite pattern we are currently working on has developed from our shared love of stones and minerals.

One of our success stories is reupholstering vintage furniture in our contemporary fabrics. Each piece needs to work in a domestic environment which is why there are so many sofas here right now! Putting them in context helps us to work out if a design is going to be successful or not.

We find London very exciting; it is the most multi-cultural city in the world and offers an unrivalled sense of freedom. When we came here in 2006, we felt really welcomed and encouraged by the fashion industry. To this day, Londoners are ready to try something new – they have a strong identity and welcome boldness and difference. London has also become an incredible place to find exotic food. This is a very Turkish area, so we can buy everything we need from the local shops. It's all right on our doorstep!

RETHINKERS

MARIA SPEAKE AND ADAM HILLS, MARYLEBONE

I was born and brought up in Oxford and then moved to Scotland. Adam and I met at Glasgow School of Art, where we were both studying architecture. Glasgow in the late 1980s and early 1990s was fun, edgy and exciting. Adam bought one of those wonderful tenement flats and we stayed there for nine years before coming to London in 1997.

Adam and I moved straight into this flat, which is where he was brought up. Frankly, I never wanted to live in London and am only still here because of this place. In the 1970s Adam's father designed everything – from the architecture to the carpet, the textiles, and the tiled bathroom. It was very ahead of its time – David Hicks meets Barcelona Pavilion, with a bit of porn thrown in – and all at the top of an Edwardian mansion block! For us the huge question was how could we change it, and did we dare?

With children in mind, the first thing I did was create a larger kitchen so that I could have the doors open to the roof garden and keep an eye on the boys, who had a sand pit there. The renovation of the apartment was fun, affordable, easy and minimal fuss.

The roof garden gives us breathing space; we have long west light up here and there is so much sky, yet everywhere you look there are chimney pots. When the boys were small, we would see the same heron flying into Regent's Park to roost every night.

At around the same time as we were redoing the flat, Adam and I were working out whether we wanted to carry on running Retrouvius, the salvage company we started in Glasgow in 1993. We were definitely early with the idea of reuse and recognising the arrogance of how easily materials were being dismissed to landfill. Back then, I don't think there were enough people in the building and design industries linking up the consequences.

Over the years I have been increasingly frustrated by salvaged materials not being used in interesting ways. As a result, I have allowed myself to be shoehorned into becoming an interior/architectural designer. Originally, I just wanted to encourage people to question how they might reduce the waste of perfectly good resources.

Home reflects so much of who you are as a person. For me, it has two meanings: there is home in terms of what I do to help other people make their spaces more interesting, and home in terms of the place I live with my family. Our home is experimental; I often use it as a canvas to try things out, which means that it will never be quite as relaxed or as comforting as other people's homes are for them. It's possibly more original, though.

Some people love the process of change in their home, while others worry that it means sweeping family references aside. In my view memories will remain, even in a new incarnation, because you are the same person living in that same space. Here, high above the London rooftops, I have many layers of memories.

MAN ABOUT TOWN

TOMASZ STARZEWSKI, SOUTH KENSINGTON

As a child of Polish parents, who were political refugees at the end of the Second World War and were granted asylum here in England, and then growing up in a very Anglo-Saxon landscape, identity is an interesting concept for me. This dual heritage made it all the more important that I claim my own visual identity.

Post-war South Kensington was known as 'mini Poland' and its three landmarks still remain: the Brompton Oratory, which for war *immigrés* and their descendants, represents the first Polish parish; the Polish Club on Exhibition Road; and most important of all, Daquise, the Polish restaurant in Thurloe Street – my weekly local.

By extraordinary coincidence, I live in the same Victorian stucco terrace as my father did in the late 1940s, when he read architecture at Imperial College. My home is a basement flat that appalled him. By then a successful Brutalist architect, he felt it to be a poor investment. Yet, as a young man, how else could I have afforded a place with its own front door and courtyard garden, as well as a forty-foot drawing room with two fireplaces and magnificent high ceilings? Despite my father's horror, I consider 'living underground', as he put it, to be very enjoyable. My father wanted my brother and I to join his architectural practice, but I felt destined to be a fashion designer. Yet, in the last decade I have been blessed with a second career as an interior designer; I owe this not only to my father, but of course to my flat.

Architects leave behind the bricks and mortar of which we are temporary custodians. This building dates from around 1886 and was converted into flats in the 1920s. In its 100-year existence as a flat, I am only the third inhabitant of this basement.

Originally, I asked my great friend and adopted mother, Tessa Kennedy – who is a 'grand' decorator in the real sense of the word – to help me to create a backdrop for the things I had collected and inherited. Tessa was my mentor, teaching me the importance of scale and that there is no such thing as an imperfect space. By creating illusion with paint effects and textures to reflect my Central European background – we Poles are the orientalists of Europe – Tessa boldly introduced colours and textiles to satisfy my Ottoman predilection. When I moved in, what is now my bedroom would have been the original Art Deco kitchen, and my bed where the Aga would have sat. To the rear of the flat, I have retained the original Art Deco bathroom and converted the coal cellars under the pavement into a new kitchen.

Living here for nearly thirty years, I have fallen in and out of love with this flat several times, redone the space on numerous occasions, and have come to the conclusion that it will always be a showcase for my design ideas, which – like me – have reached maturity and confidence.

There is something very intimate and healing about this flat. Over the years it has been a sanctuary not just for me but also for my friends. Many an emotion has been shared here. I feel blessed to have this one constant in my life – a little bit of paradise hidden away in a very personal part of London.

CREATIVE WORKS

TOM BARTLETT, NORTH KENSINGTON

I was born in London and my parents still live in the lovely house just off Ladbroke Grove where I grew up. In those days Notting Hill was bohemian rather than fancy, which fostered a sense of independence and freedom that I think is peculiarly British – we are a strange country on the edge of a civilised continent!

I often think back to my childhood when I would walk home from school and look into the windows of the Victorian houses I passed. The front rooms were all the same size and shape, yet each had been treated differently. I was fascinated by the way people lived, which is perhaps why I went on to become an architect and interior designer.

I bought this place, which was formerly a factory and then an Indian spice warehouse, in 1999. It was derelict when I stumbled across it. I worked on it for eighteen months and its bones are essentially the same today, but I have laid it out quite strangely. There is a yard at the front, and the original double-height doors lead into a small hall, through to a cavernous sitting room. The interior is not all on one floor; there is a guest bedroom and my room up separate staircases, with the kitchen and study below them. When my son, Bluey, arrived, I knocked through into next door, which required changing the layout of the kitchen and reorientating the stairs.

Although I now know that lighting, and its placement, are key to good design, I didn't have a clue when I started working on this place! I combined skylights in the roof with downlighters in the living area, which absolutely did not work! The downlighting has since been replaced by table lamps that cast pools of light and make the room cosy, despite its double height. Deciding where I wanted to sit reinforced the need for a fireplace as a focal point, while some of the furniture is an accumulation of stuff from other jobs that clients no longer wanted.

The first phase of decorating was very simple – I didn't have any money so the scheme was white. I threw in some colour during its most recent iteration, which was about four years ago. It was amazing how it changed the space. You can see by the way I dress – like a children's entertainer – that I grew up in a house that was very vibrant!

I have lived here for more than twenty years. 'Home' for me is a timeline – the layering of memories and the addition of objects that reflect passing fads. A real home should be resonant of its occupant's personality, something that we, as designers, try to recreate for our clients. I love working with people who have pictures and objects as it offers an insight into their character and provides a foundation on which to build.

Design is about a singular vision of what the whole should be. While not dismissing the importance of our British design heritage, I believe that you can be modern and soft, sympathetic and personable without resorting to tassels and the sort of decoration befitting a duke! I like to think about the future rather than try to emulate an idea of the past that is no longer truthful to our time. A home should have a delicious rhythm, be punctuated with colour and, above all, be comfortable.

RESTRAINED

WILLIAM SMALLEY, BLOOMSBURY

One of the first things you see when you walk into this house is a map of London by John Rocque, a French cartographer. The map was made in 1746 when St Paul's Cathedral was the centre of London and the first terraced blocks were being designed. This house was built in 1720, and the end of the street was the edge of London. Berkeley Square to the west was under construction, there was Mile End Road to the east and a few areas south of the river where there were bridges or crossings. There was no suburb.

The whole of this estate is owned by Rugby School in Warwickshire, which was founded in the sixteenth century as the result of a bequest made by Lawrence Sherriff, a Rugby-born London grocer. There is a village atmosphere here, possibly because it attracts a random mix of long-term renting tenants, something of a rarity in England where most people own their homes.

Ben Pentreath and I took on a joint lease for this building, as my home and his office, and the estate gave us money to do it up. It had been an office and was sad: the fireplaces were blocked up, and everything had been finished in the estate's colour scheme of gloss-green doors, magnolia walls and blue carpet.

It took Ben and me a couple of months to sort it out. During our second year here, we stripped the stairwell and laid stone flags in the entrance hall, which now look as if they have always been there. I took up the carpets everywhere else and scrubbed four floorboards every morning before going to work. They are unfinished and lovely as a result.

Ben is giving up one of the grand rooms, which he uses for meetings, and I am excited about gaining the extra space. With its panelled walls and beautiful plaster ceiling it will become a reading room, a quiet place for study. Having an extra room will be a nice change and will alter the rhythm of the flat.

When I first moved here, my worldly goods consisted of a chair, a rug, a bed and a chest of drawers, all of which I was able to fit into a small car. I don't care much about possessions, which is probably why I am not fussed about owning a home. There's a Chinese proverb, 'Let your boat of life float lightly in case your possessions sink you', which I think is very apt. Although now that I have a grand piano and a sofa, I am sunk.

An architect's role is to problem-solve. I care about creating beautiful spaces that reveal the person who lives in them and feels spatially right. There is a sensitivity involved in meeting a client's needs and making sure that they chime with my own – the two must be in harmony or the dynamic won't work.

The psyche of home and our relationship with it is complex. A home should provide shelter and retreat. I am careful about keeping my mind and my life simple. I want to be in the moment, enjoying the fall of light on a wall or the blossom changing. I live in a bubble in the centre of London where noise is absent, and I have sacrificed home ownership for quality of life. I couldn't contemplate having to move out.

RAREFIED CURIOSITIES

EMMA HAWKINS, NOTTING HILL

I was born in Australia, where I also grew up. My father is English and an antiques dealer, and my mother is an artist. As a child I remember everything in our house being for sale, so it's not surprising that I went on to become a dealer.

Up until my mid-teens, my father would bring me to the UK every three years. We would go to Scotland, which I like to think he gifted to me as it is still in my blood. My interest in the natural world is also down to my father, although I believe we are born with it. I have always been obsessed by the tactility of my surroundings, even the air I breathe on a cold morning walk. Life is not permanent, and I am convinced that our evolution, like any other animal, ends in extinction.

When I was seventeen, I moved to the UK on a permanent basis. In the 1990s I had a shop on Westbourne Grove in Notting Hill, alongside David Champion and Nick Plant of Succession, out of which I sold animal artefacts, bones and fossils. Today, I have cabinets at Dover Street Market in the West End, which give me a sense that I am still a part of the commercial world.

I left London for Edinburgh twenty years ago to continue my love affair with Scotland. I always knew that I would return to Notting Hill one day, and when I did come back and saw this 200-year-old villa, I felt an overwhelming sense that it was destined to be a permanent London home for me and my boys.

I wanted to modernise the house without losing its original features, which were remarkably untouched. It has taken two years to bring it back to life, during which time the architect and I went to great lengths to replace the lath-and-plaster ceilings and restore many of the building's other historical references. The mahogany doors were made by Michael Hart, a cabinetmaker in Scotland, to which I added early brass handles purchased from Anthony Outred. Michael and I then visited the Victoria & Albert Museum to understand the correct colour the doors should be before we started polishing. I am a perfectionist, but I hope that my attention to detail (which is probably annoying to most!) is reflected in the quality of the house, where nothing is over- or under-designed.

There is something about Notting Hill, which is why I am back. It still has an earthly energy and reminds me of a time when this part of London was very 'rock 'n' roll', and I would walk down the street in my biker boots and 1920s long leather motoring jacket. That edginess is missing now, yet I am still happy here.

Home for me will probably end up being a tiny fishing hut right on the river, in Scotland. I know I shall be fighting for space there with my boys! It will be a place for play, somewhere I won't have to feel that everything has to be immaculate. One day, I will build a studio for my collection. For me, this is a breath of consciousness – life's balance. No matter how much we might love London, we definitely need an escape.

LONDON
+
COUNTRY

I grew up in the countryside and felt at home in what I thought of as 'the wild'. As an adult, I have never stopped searching for the last few untamed places in the British Isles. These include hidden spots in Devon, Wales, Shropshire, the North Country and the Scottish Highlands, especially the border between Sutherland and Caithness, where I have spent almost every year since my early childhood following the ancient sport of falconry, a family passion now pursued in earnest by my cousin Mark.

When Matilda was born, we moved from London to Devon. I wanted to be able to offer my daughter the same freedom I enjoyed as a child, and I was also keen to return to the West Country, where most of my close family still lives.

We found a vicarage on the edge of a picturesque village in an area of 'outstanding natural beauty'. Part Devon longhouse, it has a Georgian façade and a Victorian wing and is, in short, a good old muddle of English architecture. Inside, we found a celebration of the 1970s in the form of built-in furniture, carpeted floors and patterned wallpaper.

Transforming the house has been a gradual process. Over the years we have replaced the cement floors with local, kiln-dried oak floorboards and put in underfloor heating in the hope of drying out the damp. We wanted to go off-grid as much as possible, so we installed solar panels, replaced the oil-fired heating with a wood pellet boiler and created underground reservoirs to catch and store rainwater. Rather than change the structure of the house, we have simplified it, and the result is a home that has adapted beautifully to the way we live.

Our approach to the restoration of the garden has been similarly sympathetic and reflects our commitment to rural life. We grow our own fruit and vegetables in the newly reinstated walled garden and have planted trees and hedgerows. We have also raised ducks and chickens, recently acquired a pony for Matilda, and have three Labradors and a cat.

As a result of our regenerative efforts, we are starting to see more birds, butterflies, grasshoppers and other insects. Our fruit, vegetables and eggs taste delicious and we are proud to be living at least a little bit sustainably, while also acknowledging how much we still have to learn.

The British countryside has so much to offer, and I feel hugely fortunate that I am able to witness the changing seasons: the snowdrops in winter, the heavy-headed poppies in summer, the electric flash of a kingfisher as it skims the river, the skeins of geese heading to their winter feeding grounds and the occasional glimpse of a roe deer as it vanishes silently into the trees.

ACQUIRING MINDS

ALASTAIR AND MEGAN HOLBERTON, KENSINGTON AND OXFORDSHIRE

I had known of Robert Kime for many years. He had a shop within walking distance of here, and I would pop in there from time to time. When our country house was finished, Megan noticed that our London place had started to look dowdy by comparison, so we asked Robert for help. He immediately knew what to do – it all felt very instinctive.

Our home in London is a semi-detached Victorian house, built around 1828. It has a north/south aspect, so while not light, it is cosy. By exaggerating its darkness, Robert transformed it into something rich and jewel-like. I had never managed to get the drawing room to work, but Robert understood how to improve it straight away. He took the mother-of-pearl colour of the 1890s fireplace and used the same tone on the walls; variations of the shade were then introduced into the upholstery, the lampshades and, of course, the textiles. It was quite brilliant.

Over time we became good enough friends with Robert for him to be able to say to Megan one day, 'Alastair has some good art, but he doesn't know how to hang.' He was right, as he was about so many things – and the way that he then put my paintings together enabled me to rediscover my art. His aim, that I love the room I am in at any given time, is something he has certainly achieved.

I bought my house in Oxfordshire forty years ago. It was a comfortable, if not particularly special, mid-1920s property in an incredible location. My children grew up here and it was a happy family house, but it faced the wrong way and didn't do the setting justice – it is high up in the Chiltern hills, surrounded by acres of woodland.

When I returned to England after several years' absence, I decided to refurbish. An architect I consulted suggested that I knock it down and start again. Initially I was shocked by the prospect, but rubble turns to regeneration, and I don't remember there being a huge sense of loss when we finally did just that. We ended up with a house that sits perfectly in its landscape, and our decision to keep the pagoda, the pool pavilion and the follies from the 'old house' provides a pleasing sense of continuity.

Building a modern house in the country is a real undertaking, particularly in England. I didn't like the design put forward by the first architect, so I turned to Lazzarini Pickering, an Italian studio, who created a building that is wonderful inside and out. The house was finished ten years ago and in 2017 we were awarded the Dedalo Minosse International Prize for commissioning it. The feel is very Japanese, which delights me. I collect Japanese prints and porcelain and love the sensibilities and harmony of much of their design.

The life we lead in the country is very different to the one we lead in London. There are woods to walk in, a place to swim, things to do in the garden and much more involvement with nature. We come here to be surrounded by the things that make us feel complete, and that's what we have.

Homes are refuges from the outside world, places of love, beauty and family. A home nurtures you in the same way as the things you collect do. For me, it is memories that are most important, and mine are stitched into the fabric of both houses.

'No matter the difference in our two properties, each has a similar theme – they have both been designed around a lifetime of collecting Asian art.'

ADVENTURERS

BLAKE AND CHAD PIKE, CHELSEA AND WILTSHIRE

A week after my thirtieth birthday, my husband Chad and I relocated from New York to London. I was pregnant with our first child and had no intention of spending more than a few years in England. I was a New Yorker and could not imagine living anywhere else. Yet after a few months, I found a softer rhythm in London. I stopped craving the frenzy and adrenaline of New York and grew to enjoy London's slower, more civilised pace. Soon, Chad and I realised that London was home, and we decided to raise our family in England.

Our family grew, and within seven years, there were six of us. While I was changing nappies and toting toddlers to playgroups, Chad pursued his passion and launched Eleven Experience, a portfolio of adventure lodges in beautiful, remote locations around the world. I created Twelve Interiors to transform these properties into inviting destinations, approaching them as I would my own home. I've always loved the English country house tradition of layered, almost cluttered interiors that deftly balance comfort and style. I sought to infuse this sensibility throughout each project, creating cosy lodges that are reminiscent of home.

Our family life in Chelsea was vibrant but cramped, and we longed for more outside space after our fourth child was born. In 2008, we drove across the English countryside, passing Stonehenge en route to Edington Priory, a 647-year-old farm deep in Wiltshire. It was the first and only property we viewed, beckoning us from the moment we ducked through its ancient doors.

The house had a soul. The Priory's history is so profound that it was hard to comprehend its evolving presence. Tucked into the north escarpment of Salisbury Plain, it was here that England became England when King Alfred defeated the Vikings in 878 AD. The ruins of Iron Age forts and the white horses carved in nearby chalk hills remind us how long this land has been inhabited. The house and adjacent church were built in 1361 by the Bonhommes, an order of French monks who resided at the Priory until Henry VIII dissolved the monasteries in 1536. Subsequently, both Jane Seymour and Catherine Parr had strong ties to the house. I love how the church bells toll throughout the night, instilling a sense of peace. I'm often asked if there are ghosts; I believe there are spirits here, but only kind-hearted ones.

Our happiest family moments have been spent in our country house. In the beginning, we camped with sleeping bags in empty rooms, and I wondered how I would ever make this historical place a home. It did not happen overnight. Instead, the rooms and gardens gradually took shape over a decade. There were successes and mistakes. I wanted to strike a balance that respected the past but reflected the present. Initially, the Priory had a narrow galley kitchen that was smaller and more cramped that my first New York City apartment. So, when English Heritage gave us permission to extend our Grade I-listed property, there was no question that we would start with the kitchen. We enlisted the help of our friend and architect, Eric J. Smith, who expertly designed a light-infused space where we cook, relax with our dogs and have lively family discussions in front of the fire. From Sunday roasts to Thanksgiving dinners, it all happens in this room.

Chad and I have had many wonderful years in London and Wiltshire. We believe that 'home' is a place where we can all be together, where family memories are created and where we are all drawn to return.

'I've always loved traditional Georgian architecture, so the idiosyncrasies of the Priory were not characteristics I openly embraced. It was the perfect foil to our classic London home, with its wonky low ceilings and quirky asymmetrical rooms.'

CURATORS

DAVID GIBSON AND JORGE PEREZ-MARTIN, CHELSEA AND GLOUCESTERSHIRE

We are very much two halves of the same story, although the articulation of the story can be as different as our nationalities and as diverse as our individual journeys.

London is a bit more about me, David. I knew this small but perfectly formed house forty years ago as a student, while sofa surfing with a friend at Imperial College. Twenty years ago, just after I met Jorge, the sale of the house had fallen through twice, and we happened to see it was back on the market. Tired and neglected, the house was owned by a family trust. It had stood empty for some time, but the dusty Cecil Beaton photographs of the family's children were still hanging on the walls of the sitting room and gave an insight into what a special home it must once have been. It had a great feel, we moved in and a couple of years later started a full refurbishment to create a London haven for us and my two sons.

The restoration involved a lot of work, but each time I crossed the threshold, I knew I wanted to be here. I found it the easiest house to be in on my own; Jorge was still living mainly in Sussex, where our antiques business was based, and my two sons were only in London periodically. When I walk through the door today, this place is more special for me than it was that first time, as the four of us now have the twenty years of the memories it has given us.

Home for me is about privacy, constancy, proximity to my favourite things and being surrounded by the people I am close to. This house has delivered all of that and I feel immensely privileged to have been the custodian.

The country house, which we bought over ten years ago, is our story, David's and mine. I am Jorge: Spanish, romantic, someone who loves the idea of home. Both David and I had comfortable and caring upbringings, but our sense of home was disrupted. We have both been on a journey to create a home that protects and cares for us both.

My life in England started in Sussex, where I opened an antiques shop in Petworth and, as a result, I began to do up other people's homes. One day I realised that I needed a new challenge, so David and I moved our country base and the antiques business to Gloucestershire.

We fell in love with this house the moment we saw it. It had not been touched since the 1980s and was in need of restoration.

No matter what improvements we make or how many twenty-first-century comforts we introduce, it is important to both of us that we do not lose the soul of this place. I prefer to get things done but accept David's view that we should take as long as we need to get the house right, which evolves around the things we both like. We don't want to fake anything, so we kept the distressed plaster walls as close to the original as possible. And we may never restore the staircase, as the longer we leave it, the more we love it! You need to see the scars of a house to understand its historical reference.

The emotional tie we feel for this house is extremely strong. For me, it's as if I was born here or have lived here before. For David, the joy of this place is in the expectation of coming home to a place that we have created together.

'Home is everything, and for us, it became increasingly important to create continuity and a legacy for the future here in the country for the next stage of our life together.'

STORYTELLERS

GABY DELLAL AND DAVID JOHNSON, NOTTING HILL AND CORNWALL

Most people have only got one design story, and mine is my love of colour and mid-century modern furniture. London has always been a part of my life; in 1984 I had a flat next door to the house we live in now, where the proportions were amazing, and I had a bright green kitchen. Notting Hill at the time was rough, trendy and full of musicians. I married and lived happily next door, later acquiring the basement, which I turned into a double-height space and extended into the garden. I admire architects, enjoy the implied discipline and the challenge of reconfiguring.

When life changed, I ended up selling that property and my three children and I moved next door. It was one of those happy chances where the move was almost imperceptible. We carried everything from one house to the other. The house was split into bedsits, and instead of working with an architect, we decided to take down the temporary partitions and breathe life back into it. With the bedsits removed, its spirit as a family house returned, peopled by the five of us as well as many dogs and friends.

We painted each room and tiled the bathroom. Ten years later, we put down a parquet floor and eventually realised that we could alter a cupboard into a shower room. The fact that we have barely changed a thing is what gives this place its authenticity and magic. It will be very hard to let go of this house because our history is embedded in its walls.

Sadly, Notting Hill has changed and become a metropolis of shopping. Gone are the lovely antiques shops where I bought most of the furniture for here. Our house is probably the only one that doesn't have railings or security gates installed. Most days, people stand and gawk at the wisteria growing up the front of the house. I like to believe there is a scent of real life that seeps out of our home that attracts people to it. Now that the boys have moved out, we have friends who lodge here for long periods of time, which keeps the house alive, despite the changing population of the neighbourhood.

My mornings in Cornwall begin with a swim. I miss the sea enormously when I leave, not just the swimming, but falling asleep to the sound of the waves beyond my bedroom window. The beach here is the most beautiful in the world – even Greece can't compare – and the view from our living room changes every five minutes.

Until the 1940s, this area of Cornwall was mined for copper and tin. If you look at the cliffs you can see the scars of ruined chimney stacks and the remains of an aqueduct. There was once a harbour here, too, where boats would arrive from Wales and exchange their cargoes of coal for ore. The harbour wall has disappeared and the nose of the cliff below us has fallen off. One day, I guess, our seventeenth-century cottage will simply slip into the sea.

Before we bought this place, it was lived in by the local hotel manager and consisted of little more than a kitchen and a living room. We extended it, with the help of an architect, and salvaged much of the furniture and furnishings from reclamation yards.

There was a time when I rented out this place, but it feels too personal to keep doing that. The boys love it here and we try to visit as much as we can. Cornwall is the place where they surf and I go swimming, and London is the place where we light a fire!

'When I leave London for Cornwall, it only takes a couple of days before I feel as if I have been on holiday. It's something about the sea and the air.'

FREE SPIRIT

JANE ORMSBY GORE, KILBURN AND WALES

I have a conflicted relationship with London – I dread coming to town, yet when I get here I find that I rather like it. I have always lived in other people's houses. This flat, which has been my home for the past twelve years, belongs to my friend Anita, who takes care of my finances. My friends and family call me a 'homing bird', but I find that as long as the place I am living in is comfortable, welcoming, colourful and relaxing, I am happy. All it took to personalise this place was a coat of paint, a few pictures and some textiles. I also have the luxury of a door that opens onto a small back garden, enough for a fox to feel sufficiently at home to spend the night in my dog's basket in the kitchen!

Christopher Gibbs, a lifelong friend, undoubtedly had the greatest influence on me. He gave me a job in his shop in Islington and took me to see endless houses and churches. He was always curious and his unique way of looking at things showed me what was important. After leaving Christopher's, I worked for *Vogue* and then moved to the country to bring up my four children. As they were growing up, I opened a shop in my local town of Oswestry, and then one in London on the Wandsworth Bridge Road called Fieldhouse, selling kitchen things, Le Creuset and pretty china.

When finally I returned to London to work as a decorator, I spent ten years with David Mlinaric, who has been a great friend since the 1960s and with whom I am wonderfully still working.

When living in London finally proved too much for me, I returned home to Wales. A few people I had met through David started asking for things to be done to their houses. Inevitably, I was drawn back to London where I rented a place from John Michell,

another friend. The flat was just one room, with a kitchen, bathroom and a tiny room under the stairs that I used as an office when I started my own business.

I have no idea how I ended up as a decorator, for I am not a Nicky Haslam, who I have known since he was at school with my brother and love dearly. My style is spontaneous, instinctive and comes from the heart. I had always decorated for myself using colour and textiles, and I tell other people's stories the same way.

I was born five miles from where I find myself now and have lived in Wales all my life. For a while, home was the farm on the estate where I grew up. It was meant to be temporary, but it had so much going for it that it was hard to find something else as good. I needed outbuildings, sheds and a property with its own water source. Then, more than twenty years ago, I found a mill house. It is impossible to describe the state it was in when I bought it – no love, no rhythm, no poetry, no flow …

I needed help, so I asked a lovely man called Gerald Skelton, who had always done odd jobs for me. Initially, I just wanted him to take out the dreadful fitted kitchen, but he liked coming to the house and ended up doing everything – from the kitchen and the stables to the fireplaces and the roof. He died sitting at my kitchen table, passionate to the end.

I am a country girl who happened to grow up in a big house. When I am asked to do a decorating job, I think about the spaces and build them up slowly in my head – none is ever a complete picture. I take my cue from nature. The steep hillsides and deep valleys of the Welsh countryside are spectacular and have always been my inspiration.

'I take my lessons from nature. My sense of colour, my personal history and reference are all here, in Wales.'

AESTHETE

JASPER CONRAN, BAYSWATER AND DORSET

I had a peripatetic childhood. My parents divorced when I was a baby and there followed several different marriages which meant my being moved around a lot. I do have fond memories of a lovely house in Regent's Park, though.

I have lived in this flat for twenty-two years. Over time, it has changed from being an elegant but rather austere set piece to what you see now.

I was initially drawn to the flat's sense of space and its high-ceilinged rooms. It wasn't a wreck, but it was done up in a style which had to go! When I first came here, the double doors that open onto the drawing room were blocked off and the drawing room was my bedroom. I have since swapped the rooms around and opened everything up.

Prior to moving here, I lived in Primrose Hill, Regent's Park and South Kensington. A few years ago, I got married and it has changed my life for the better.

A new phase of decorating is opening up here following the acquisition of the floor above. It is going to be more modern in terms of the artwork and possibly furniture. When my father died, I realised that I had never wanted to compete with him; modernism has never figured in any of my homes, so I am coming to the party rather late!

Over the course of my life, I have had the good luck to live in the most extraordinary houses in the country, which, for one reason or another, did not work out. In one instance, it was a lack of neighbours; I had bought a beautiful house in Suffolk but it was too far away for people to feel they could just drop in. As a result, I was either rattling around there on my own or I was running a hotel.

The place where I now live with my husband, Oisin, is perfect. I have no intention of moving, ever. The house belonged to my stepmother, Caroline, who was very happy here until her partner died, and she decided to sell. When she told me her plan, I realised that I could not bear the idea of her letting Bettiscombe go out of the family.

I had never cast a proprietorial eye on this house, yet I had stayed here a lot and always loved it. I think Caroline was thrilled when I offered to buy Bettiscombe. My whole family comes to stay and there is a sense of continuity – it's still a family house!

Working up the interior here – layering it and then stripping it back – has become a personal journey for me. It's as if I am painting my own life. Now that I am married, the meaning of home has been defined at last: it is me, Oisin and my dog, Minnow. This house has proved to be very settling. I am content.

'I have always thought that time gives an object soul, and my London flat and Dorset manor house are the backdrops to a lifetime's collection of Elizabethan portraits, as well as furniture that has mellowed over the years and that I cannot bear to be parted from.'

THE COLLECTORS' COLLECTOR

SIMON UPTON

BELGRAVIA AND NORFOLK

Great design stands the test of time, and the day I arrived to photograph this majestic Regency terraced house my sense of anticipation was keen. While I had photographed John Stefanidis's work in the past, I was well aware that this was considered to be one of his finest – a project he undertook more than forty years ago. Built in the 1840s, the house had been a series of offices for nearly half a century. Transforming it into a family home must have been a Herculean task. Not only was the building gutted and rebuilt, but Stefanidis revealed his creative genius with a grand, columned entrance hall, a new stone staircase with a neoclassical balustrade and a light-filled swimming pool in the basement, which at the time must have been one of the first of its kind in central London.

All these years later the interior has remained timeless, testimony to the fact that Stefanidis is considered to be one of the greatest designers of the twentieth century. A careful restoration is underway, and Philip Hooper, now with Colefax & Fowler but who worked with Stefanidis on the house in the 1980s, was asked to tidy it up a bit. At the same time, Tomasz Starzewski immersed himself in Stefanidis's archives, researching fabrics and reweaving carpets for certain rooms, to maintain Stefanidis's original vision. Everything had to be replicated exactly.

For me, the triumph of this wonderful house is the drawing room, where Stefanidis had the walls painted with a floral motif from an eighteenth-century fabric on a beautiful turquoise background. Unrestored, the colour is still glorious today and an unexpected counterpoint to the collection of contemporary paintings, sculptures and objects that fills the room.

I found the house in Norfolk to be a delightful contrast to the grandeur of London, and a Garland Necklace sculpture by Owen Bullett on the lawn just the precursor to the art I was soon to discover inside.

Hooper was tasked with finding a version of country living that would afford more space for the collection. One of the criteria was to find a location east of Hackney, an area with apparently the greatest concentration of artists in the world. Over the years, Hooper had worked on a number of projects in Norfolk and Suffolk and was able to take advantage of local knowledge in the search.

By all accounts, it was a typical, tired country house. A few structural things needed doing, but the bones of the house were solid. Hooper has a reputation for his ability to create a balance in interior architecture, and with the help of an historic buildings consultant, he was able to unpick some of the internal structure and create a gallery space in the attic. The footprint of the house was kept to its basic form, reallocating some of the back of house space to allow for a better kitchen area, while creating further outbuildings, as well as an art store, all in a quiet, seamless extension.

Hooper worked with the collector on the colours for the house – the 'Cucumber' green of the entrance hall, for example, was one he had always wanted to try out – while the lime green in the principal bedroom is in homage to David Hicks. As extravagant marble bathrooms or grand decorating gestures were incompatible with the simplicity of this house, Hooper was able to repurpose some items from London, approaching the decoration with a sense of fun and allowing this amazing collection to speak for itself.

'John Stefanidis and Philip Hooper have each created a harmonious backdrop to a wonderful collection of art and ceramics.'

INFORMED

ROGER JONES AND GREGORY CHAMBERS, CHELSEA AND WALES

The architects who designed this building in 1936 had a very specific objective in mind, that each flat and studio should be a home as well as a place to live. It was marketed under the banner: 'Chesil Court – where you would like to live!'

The sixty-eight flats are all of modest proportions and were originally designed as rentals for professionals. Essentially Art Deco in style, it is an iconic building, solid and well-built, and any change to the structure of the flats requires permission from the management company.

Greg and I had sold our home in Kensington but had not set our hearts on a particular period property with which to replace the view we had enjoyed. When we saw Chesil Court, we became so hooked on the building – it is particularly pretty at night with all the lights sparkling – that we ended up buying a flat here.

We didn't really alter the layout apart from turning the bathroom into a shower room and installing double doors between the bedroom and the living room. We carried out a thorough renovation, re-plastering the walls and stripping the Crittall windows before repainting them.

Although flats in this block continue to be much sought after – people seem to like its slightly small scale and 1930s charm – our flat is too compact to ever really be home. It's a place to perch rather than a place to settle.

Home for me is Wales. I am Welsh. My grandmother was born twenty miles away, so I feel a connection to this area. The space and the fact that we are surrounded by beautiful countryside are the main reasons we moved here.

I was looking for an old house that would be a bit of a project. One day, in 2003, I went to an exhibition in Cardiff of paintings by the eighteenth-century Welsh landscape artist Thomas Jones. Inspired, we spent the rest of the day exploring the area, which I hadn't visited since I was a child. Suddenly, I felt at home and said to Greg: 'Let's look for our next country house in Wales.'

The house we found is a mixture of styles: it started life as a sixteenth/seventeenth-century barn, was turned into a modest rectory in 1780 and then extended, in an ad hoc fashion, throughout the following century. There are things of real architectural interest here.

Although the house was falling down and therefore ticked my box as a project, I did not feel that the layout needed altering or reordering. All the rooms have kept their original functions, apart from the former dining room which we now use as a library and the original kitchen becoming our dining room. The rather charming lean-to conservatory was so dilapidated we had to demolish it, so we asked architect Craig Hamilton to design an extension to the hall instead.

I am not a knowledgeable gardener, but it has been great fun working with the terrain here. Although the house is perched on the edge of a steep slope, we have been able to create a garden of grass and topiary which I enjoy immeasurably.

The house is full of things I have collected over the years, which makes me feel grounded and comfortable. I love our flat in Chelsea, but when I get to Wales, I have a sense of connection and belonging that I don't have in London.

'Priorities change as you get older! We exchanged a larger flat in London for a small pied-à-terre, and a cottage in Wiltshire for a grander house in Wales.'

CLASS ACT

TISH WEINSTOCK AND TOM GUINNESS, HOLLAND PARK AND WILTSHIRE

I always thought London had everything I needed, but that was before we found our house in the country. When Tom and I met, I had a basement flat in Notting Hill and he lived in East London. This mews house, which needed a lot of work, was our first home together. My stepfather and a local architect helped us to reimagine what turned out to be a four-year project. I remember going to site meetings and realising I didn't really know what I was doing. Our son Reuben arrived before the house was finished, so Tom's sister took us in. I have very fond memories of that time.

Initially, I wanted nothing to do with the interior. Then a friend introduced me to Rachel Chudley, at which point I swiftly concluded that I did care about how the inside of the house was going to take shape. In the end it became a collaborative effort between me, Rachel and Tom. It was an amazing learning curve for us. The more experience we gained, the more we understood how to live in a particular space, which gave us the confidence to try to do our country house on our own.

I grew up having to go to the country every weekend just when the social action in London was kicking off. I felt like I was missing out and for years afterwards, I associated the country with somewhere I did not want to be! Of course, as soon as I had Reuben, my feelings changed. I think one's attitude towards the countryside depends on what stage you are at in life. At the moment, spending weekends in Wiltshire and weekdays in London works for me.

We looked for a place in Wiltshire because it made sense for us to be near both our families. The Guinness clan live in Biddesden, and my mother and two sisters also live locally.

It didn't take long to make the house work. Practical help came in the form of Fiona Shelborne, a lifelong friend of my family's. Although I knew what I liked, I didn't know my pelmets from my swags – unlike Fiona, who does speak decorating language! Interior design becomes obsessive and I now understand how grandees such as John Stefanidis, Nicky Haslam, David Mlinaric and Robert Kime live on through the likes of Tom and me, who continue to appreciate their extraordinary talents.

This house does not have high ceilings or beautiful mouldings. The detailing has been done quite crudely, which has enabled us to add to it without it being inappropriate. I love dark, opulent colours that bring a gothic feel, while Tom prefers a more minimalist approach.

When we are here, we do the same things every weekend, which I find really comforting. Home means so many different things for Tom and me. It is the physical space in which we live, the backdrop to our relationship and a reflection of our shared tastes and interests.

'I like to think that our house in London and our house in the country reflect both our styles, which are evolving all the time.'

ACKNOWLEDGEMENTS

First and foremost, I would like to thank Karen Howes, my agent and friend. She has been my guide, editor and compass on so much of my professional journey.

My thanks to all at Vendome Press, especially Beatrice Vincenzini, and to designer Peter Dawson (Grade Design) for his eye and expertise, without which the book would not look as it does. To Sara Mathers for her input and keen eye, to Tom Teasdale and Socrates Mitsios, my photo team, and to Nicky Haslam for his kind foreword.

This book would be nothing without all the contributors: Tom Bartlett, Kate Braine, Adam Bray, Jasper Conran, Poppy Delevingne, Gaby Dellal and David Johnson, Bella Freud, David Gibson and Jorge Perez-Martin, Emma Hawkins, Alastair and Megan Holberton, Roger Jones and Gregory Chambers, Jane Ormsby Gore, Blake and Chad Pike, Joanna and Nick Plant, William Smalley, Maria Speake and Adam Hills, Tomasz Starzewski, John Stefanidis, Francis Upritchard and Martino Gamper, Christopher de Vos and Peter Pilotto, Tish Weinstock and Tom Guinness, and Hubert Zandberg.

I would also like to thank *The World of Interiors, Architectural Digest, House & Garden, Vogue, Tatler* and *Harper's Bazaar,* as well as their editors and commissioning editors: Anna Wintour, Hamish Bowles, Emily Tobin, Amy Astley, Michael Shome, Hatta Byng, Emily Senior, Liz Elliot, David Nicholls, Richard Dennen, Eva de Romarate, Lydia Slater and Sian Parry. Additional thanks must also go to Min Hogg, Rupert Thomas, Mark Lazenby and to the wider '*World of Interiors* family', and also to Sue Crewe. You have all been instrumental in my success as an interiors and lifestyle photographer.

To my wife, Anne, and daughter, Matilda, who encourage and inspire me.

A final thanks to London itself, which has been my base and the 'jumping-off place' for my career as a photographer for the past thirty years.

PICTURE CREDITS

Page No
2/3   Designer: Jasper Conran
4/5   Interior designer: Joanna Plant
6/7   Interior architect and designer: John Stefanidis
       Artists: Owen Bullett, Ian Jones, Marina Kappos, Chun Liao, Maria Militsi, Magdalene Odundo, Lawson Oyekan, Jim Partridge, Henry Pim, Sarah Radstone, Nick Rena, Richard Slee
8   Architect: William Smalley
       Furniture designer: Hans Wegner
10   Interior designer: Jane Ormsby Gore
13   Interior decorator: Nicky Haslam
14   Interior designer: Robert Kime
16   Interior designer (*above*): Roger Banks-Pye, Colefax & Fowler
16   Interior designer (*below*): Rose Uniacke
17   Interior designer: Rose Uniacke
18   Interior designer: Robert Kime
19   Liza Bruce and Nicholas Alvis Vega
20   *Below*: Peter Hone
20&21   Will and Charlotte Fisher, Jamb

HUNTER GATHERER
Interior designer: Hubert Zandberg Interiors
Artists: Billy Childish, Edith Dekyndt, Kaye Donachie, Kay Harwood, Ben Mclaughlin, Teo Soriano, Sebastian Stöhrer, Mario Testino
Furniture designers: Enrique Garcel, Pia Manu, Carlo Mollino, Danielle Quarante
Hand-painted decorative border: Anna Glover

INFLUENTIAL GLAMOUR
Architect: Alex Tart Architects
Interior designer: Joanna Plant

RACONTEUR
Interior designer & antiques dealer: Adam Bray

ENIGMA
Interior architect: Maria Speake
Artists: Bruce Bernard, Lucien Freud, Sarah Lucas, Nigel Shafran

ART & DESIGN
Furniture designers: Franco Albini, Martino Gamper, Max Lamb
Artists: Stuart Cumberland, Laura Gannon, Luke Gottelier, Peter McDonald, Ruthanne Tudball, Francis Upritchard

DESIGN DUO
Interior designer: Joanna Plant
Antiques dealer: Nick Plant
Artists: Lucy Naughton
Furniture designers: J&J Kohn, Otto Wagner
Lighting designers: Arne Jacobsen

GRANDEE
Interior architect and designer: John Stefanidis

ARTIST IN RESIDENCE
Interior designer: Christophe Gollut
Artists: Lauren Bauer, Kate Braine, Tancredi di Carcaci, Robin Cawdron-Stewart, Aigana Gali, Joyce Gascoigne, Takashi Murakami, Nuala O'Donovan, Annamaria Succi

INTERIOR DRESSERS
Architect: Claudio Silvestrin
Textile designers: Christopher de Vos and Peter Pilotto – PPCDV
Artists: Luke Gottelier
Tapestry by Kumi Sugai
Custom quilted and embroidered textile cushions from PPCDV
Furniture designers: Percival Lafer, Max Lamb, PPCDV, Claudio Silvestrin
Lighting designers: Bethan Laura Wood

RETHINKERS
Architect: Nicholas Hills
Interior and architectural designer: Maria Speake
Architectural reclamation & design: Retrouvious, Adam Hills
Artists: Jean Lurçat
Furniture designers: Marcel Breuer, Antonio Citterio, A J Milne
Lighting designers: Pierre Guariche

MAN ABOUT TOWN
Tomasz Starzewski: interior designer
Artists: Mathew Bray & Matthew Collins, Owen Bullett, Damien Elwes, Yoyoi Kusama, Wotjek Starzewski
Furniture designers: Oriel Harwood
Textiles: Surekha Jain, by Walid

CREATIVE WORKS
Architect & interior designer: Tom Bartlett, Waldo Works

RESTRAINED
Architect: William Smalley
Artists: Antony Gormley, Olivia Horley, F L Kennet, Victor Pasmore, Margo Selby, Rupert Spira, Marc Vaux, Edmund de Waal
Furniture designers: Antonio Citterio for B&B Italia, Muller Van Severen, Hans Wegner

RAREFIED CURIOSITIES
Interior designer & antiques dealer: Emma Hawkins
Artists: Callum Innes, Clementine Keith-Roach, Tarka Kings,
Furniture designers: Michael Hart

ACQUIRING MINDS
Interior designer: Robert Kime
Architect: Lazzarini Pickering

ADVENTURERS
Interior designer: Blake Pike
Architect: Eric J Smith
Artists: Francisco Bores, Walton Ford, Sarah Graham, David Montgomery

CURATORS
David Gibson and Jorge Perez-Martin, Brownrigg Antiques, www.brownrigg.co.uk
Artists: Luke Edward Hall
Furniture designers: Pierre Jeanneret, Gilbert Poillerat
Bespoke hand-stitched cushions: Paul Bailey @ thismanswork
Bespoke hand-painted lampshades: Alvaro Picardo @by.alvaro.picardo
Wallpaper – Jet by Whiteworks
Hand-painted wall finishes Magda Gordon

STORYTELLERS
Interior designer: Gaby Dellal
Artists: Ian Hamilton Finlay, Hylton Nel

FREE SPIRIT
Interior decorator: Jane Ormsby Gore
Artists: Peter Hone, Ramona Rainey, Michael Wishart
Lighting: Katherine Shells for JR Design

AESTHETE
Designer: Jasper Conran
Artists: Oisin Byrne, Gary Farrelly, Howard Hodgkin

THE COLLECTORS' COLLECTOR
Interior architect & designer: John Stefanidis (Belgravia)
Interior designer: Philip Hooper, Colefax & Fowler (Norfolk)
Artists: Craigie Aitchison, Leonor Antunes, Gordon Baldwin, Barnaby Barford, Tord Boontje, Mattia Bonetti, Kasper Bosmans, Sebastian Brajkovic, Alison Britton, Owen Bullett, Hugh Byrne, Luke Caulfield, David Clark, Philip Eglin, James Evans, Rainer Fetting, Kevin Gallagher, Paul Harbutt, Ewen Henderson, Kerry Jameson, Ian Jones, Marina Kappos, Chun Liao, Maria Loboda, Marvin Maciejowski, Baraj Matthews, Carol McNicoll, Nao Matsunaga, Maria Militsi, Magdalene Odundo, Lawson Oyekan, Henry Pim, Sarah Radstone, Nick Rena, James Rigler, Richard Slee, Paul Storey, Henry Taylor, Joanna Vasconcelos, Adrian Wisniewski

INFORMED
Interior designer: Roger Jones, Colefax & Fowler

CLASS ACT
Interior designer: Rachel Chudley (Holland Park)
Interior designer: Fiona Shelborne (Wiltshire)

LONDON LIVING
First published in 2023 by The Vendome Press
Vendome is a registered trademark of The Vendome Press LLC

VENDOME PRESS US
PO Box 566
Palm Beach, FL 33480

VENDOME PRESS UK
Worlds End Studio
132–134 Lots Road
London, SW10 0RJ

www.vendomepress.com

Distributed in North America by Abrams Books
Distributed in the United Kingdom, and the rest of the world, by Thames & Hudson

Every effort has been made to identify and contact all copyright holders and to obtain
their permission for the use of any copyrighted material. The publisher apologizes for
any errors or omissions and would be grateful if notified of any corrections that should
be incorporated in future reprints or editions of this book.

ISBN 978-0-86565-430-3

Publishers: Beatrice Vincenzini, Mark Magowan, and Francesco Venturi
Editor: Karen Howes
Creative Direction: Sara Mathers
Production Director: Jim Spivey
Designer: Peter Dawson, www.gradedesign.com

Library of Congress Cataloging-in-Publication Data available upon request.

Printed and bound in China by RR Donnelley (Guangdong)
Printing Solutions Company Ltd.

FIRST PRINTING